Penned Up:
Writing Out the Pandemic

Penned Up:
Writing Out the Pandemic

poems

from the Applegate Poets

Lisa E Baldwin
Diana Coogle
Beate Foit
Seth Kaplan
H. Ní Aódagaín
Joan Peterson
Christin Lore Weber

N8tive Run Press
Jerome Prairie, Oregon

First Printing

ISBN 978-0-578-31512-6

Published by N8tive Run Press

N8tive Run Press
— a subsidiary of N8tive Run Enterprises
5007 Laurel Avenue
Grants Pass, Oregon 97527

n8tiverun.enterprises@gmail.com

Photo credits:
front cover, photo of Upper Squaw Lake by Marion Hadden
back cover, group photo by Lily Myers Kaplan

Contents

Penned Up: Writing Out the Pandemic

Foreword

Penned Up: Writing Out the Pandemic

March 2020. A pestilence is on the land. Southern Oregon, like the rest of the country, is shut down. Restaurants and cafes have closed. The Oregon Shakespeare Festival in Ashland has closed. The Britt Festival, our summer concert series in nearby Jacksonville, has closed. Businesses have closed. Homes are suddenly too small for both Zoom meetings and online school classes. Breadmaking becomes a new hobby.

The Applegate Poets are hunkered down. We no longer meet monthly to read and discuss our poems, as we had done since 2015, when Joan Peterson, at the suggestion of Lawson Inada (Oregon poet laureate, 2016) brought our group together. Without the stimulation of monthly meetings, my poetry was sagging. Maybe that was true of the other Applegate Poets, too. Were Joan, Lisa, Beate, Ní Aódagaín, Christin, and the others in our group still writing? I didn't know. That flow of exchange had been dammed by the pestilence.

Lisa Baldwin breached the dam. She sent us an email at the end of March, suggesting we write a poem a day in April in recognition of National Poetry Month. She would send us daily prompts by email, and we would email our responses ("reply all") each day.

Five of us (plus Lisa) enthusiastically accepted the challenge. Here was a way to be productive while life was on hold. Penned up in our homes, we would take up our pens and write poems.

The creative flow was exciting, a stimulus in dull days, a way to answer and address the sadness in the world around us. It was a way to sing our songs to each other. We looked forward to the daily prompt and the responses it engendered. How would Joan interpret a prompt to write about Paul Revere's ride? What family story would Ní Aódagaín tell?

Then April came to an end, and the poem-a-day came to an end, but the pandemic was not at an end. Still ensconced in our homes, we missed our daily exchange of poetry and the intimacy we had experienced through that sharing. We wanted to continue, but maybe not at that pace; not a poem a day, but maybe, Ní Aódagaín suggested, a poem a week, with a different person each week giving the prompt.

And so, week by week, the prompts came in. Some challenged us to write in a form: a sonnet, a golden shovel, a sijo, a pantoum. Some suggested a topic: a journey, a dream, role models, a hike. Some were specific: write in response to Annie Dillard's essay "Living like Weasels"; write a poem to put in a bottle and cast on the sea. We were asked to write a recipe for something, to write a poem using twelve of thirty given words, to write in response to a painting or to a piece of music. Some prompts responded to the season, others to current events. Each week brought a new challenge to our creative imaginations.

Late summer brought more challenges, of a different kind. As if the pandemic weren't enough, wildfires swept through our communities and mountain forests. The Almeda Fire destroyed many homes in communities close to the Applegate, and fires deeper in the mountains threatened some of our own homes. Smoke descended over the valley, shutting us all indoors even more tightly than the pandemic had done and casting a pall over already burdened spirits.

Add to those two traumas the tension of the 2020 Presidential election, and you have a perfect storm of anxiety, despair, and despondency. But as the days and months of the *annus horribilis* wore on, the Applegate Poets continued to find, in our shared poetry, both solace and inspiration, voiced, from time to time, in an email:

Lisa: "This poetry potlatch we have going is the most nourishing, soul-sustaining 'gathering' I can imagine in this locked-down, isolating world we are in."

Ní Aódagaín: "In this time of such upheaval, fear, and sorrow I am so, so grateful that I have you all as a circle of friends. Your beautiful words uplift and inspire."

Beate: "I draw hope from all our poems. They help me cope."

Joan: "Thank you, everyone, for your extremely inspiring poems!"

Christin: "This was a really difficult week for me, and your poems did so much to re-balance me."

On the eve of the New Year, as we looked into the future, we could see brightness ahead. Communities were rebuilding after the fires. The COVID vaccine was on its way. It wouldn't be long, we thought, before we could meet in person—masked, outdoors, socially distanced. Finally, in March 2021, we met at a winery on the Applegate River to enjoy a glass of wine and share our poems on the shores of the river. A new member, Seth, was with us.

April 2021. Oregon is beginning to open up. The restrictions of the pandemic have lifted. The Oregon Shakespeare Festival has announced a live performance in the outdoor theater later in the summer. People are flocking to cafes, sitting outdoors in restaurants. People are getting vaccinated. Gradually the pandemic is losing its fight. Life is returning to what it used to be, though with the difference of the pandemic's scars and its still-hovering, though diminished, presence. It's National Poetry Month again, and, again, Lisa challenges us to write a poem a day. Again we are penning poetry like mad. This April our spirits, like our domestic lives, are feeling freer again.

At the end of April 2021, we each had one hundred and two new poems from the past thirteen months—or presumably; some of us had missed a week or a day now and then, and our newest member had far fewer. Some of the poems were throw-aways (but they were written; they answered the prompt!); some were gems; some were still unpolished but potential gems.

By this time the Applegate Poets had been sharing their poems with each other for six years. In years past we had had Valentine's Day readings at the Applegate Library, Christmas-season readings at Pacifica Gardens. As poets, each of us had matured and deepened. In April of 2021, Ní Aódagaín broached the idea that we create a book of poems by these six Applegate Poets who had shared their poems with each other during the thirteen months of the pandemic, plus Seth who had joined us towards the end of that time. Lisa took over leadership of the project, offering publication through her company, N8tive Run Press.

Thus the book in your hands.

Penned Up is a product of the shared work of the Applegate Poets and of Lisa Baldwin's editorial and production oversight. Here you will find Christin Lore Weber's strong spiritual voice, as in "Father Mother God," and Lisa Baldwin's laser-sharp, wicked-twinkle-in-the-eye language, as in "What the world needs now is." Here you will find Joan Peterson dancing with her one-year-old great-grandson ("Learning to Dance"), using the rhythm of the villanelle form to dance her images; Beate speaking for the river in an empathetic shape-shifting ("The Moldau"); Seth expressing a complex relationship with his mother—"You who fed me words/I took as nourishment"—in "Untitled & Unfinished." Here you will find Ní Aódagaín's fierce strength in seeing the political as personal ("I Am Enraged"), and my own poetry, about which another poet said, "It can be quirky and irreverent, but lurking and leaking out of the lines is a profound sense of awe and respect."

Some poems in this book are intensely personal. Some are spiritual, some humorous, some political, some thought-provoking or challenging. The poems are varied, as are the backgrounds of the poets, but we all have a love of poetry and a love of our home in the beautiful Applegate region of Southern Oregon. All of the poems come from an interior depth, the spiritual, psychological, and creative footing each of us found during the pandemic by penning poetry and sharing it with each other.

Diana Coogle
Applegate, Oregon

I

Lisa E Baldwin

Poet's Statement:

The fourteen months of lockdown isolation necessitated by the COVID-19 pandemic might have killed me as a poet were it not for the salvation found in our online poetry group. In my view, the work of a poet is to recognize poetry in the physical, living world and translate that experience into a common language. A poem conveys understanding more than knowledge, perspective more than depiction, and it seems to me that such work is impossible in isolation, impossible to know the common language of my solitary experience without some communion with others. Understanding and perspective are easily twisted and refracted in the echo chamber created by months of imposed isolation.

In selecting the poems to include in this anthology, I was struck by how often I had written about Time—the passage of time, both swift and slow; the impact of time, on hope and patience and despair; the presence of time, at once overbearing and obscure. Each of the ten poems presented here touches on some aspect of time, whether directly or indirectly. Time is the thread holding this section together.

Seven Days into April 2020

The moon was still up in the western sky
well after sunrise this morning,
broad-faced full moon, super moon,
pink moon of April, stunning
as it rose last night.
And like the seven days of April
already past and the forbearing
eternity that was March,
one day is indistinguishable
from another, time interminate
from night-to-day-
to-night-to-day-to-
night-to-day
and on.

The Permanence of Change

The best of seasons is the change,
the moving on to whatever is next.
Transition keeps us glad;
we move on from what we've had
and relish that which comes.
The space between
is breathing room,
for anything that lingers,
lingers far too long.
It makes us weary,
makes us lose our eyes
so we walk past a crowd of columbine
or miss the firs' bright growth.
We love most the new arrival
coming 'round four times each year,
sometimes earlier than expected,
sometimes fashionably late,
but always welcomed with cheer.
Nothing in nature stays the same,
the status quo can not remain.
Mountain to rock to gravel to sand,
bud to blossom to apple,
desire to child to man to dust.
The Earth revolves and all evolves,
the only permanence is change.

from The Historical Record

The first century of the Plasticene Age was marked by extreme environmental degradation and climate change due primarily to the excesses of human activity and greed. The warmer, wetter climate fostered the evolution of many new bacterium and virus; spread by unwitting and witless humans, some caused the first mass die-off of humans starting in 2020 (see also *COVID-19*). The historic pandemic coincided with global unrest and an unprecedented failure of humanity.

For a time, there was a healing pause.
                                        And the people withdrew.
            The people stepped back.

Owls and Lions came out in the daylight;

deer s a u n t e r e d like tourists
around ~~*silent*~~ Times Square.

For a time, there was a cleansing pause

<—and the skies were blue again—>

                        Has it always been more beautiful
after nightfall?   Even now a few

            stars unfade to shine.

For a time, there was a material pause.
            For a time,
                        the people stopped.

Carpe Diem: Friday, November 13

Superman's tattered cape is hung up in the scraggly
old cottonwood snag at the edge of our neighboring field,
and I think it must have been a wild black-eyed wind
to blow him and his cape out of the sky,
like the unhinged skull-knocker that blew in
this morning, scattering uncollected leaves
like airborne bones over field and forest.

And I think a day that started with a gun-shot crack
from a blown transformer in the dark morning hours
must be seized by the throat and ridden like a curve,
grasping without bias whatever miracle hand-hold you find.

I think sometimes mindlessness is
a necessity, a skill, a tool for survival
but it is not a matter
of choice, of silence, or even of will.
It takes more than will to still
this buzzing mind, so full
of shaggy, unconnected comprehensions,
of feathery vows and arrowhead promises.

I think I think too much, yet
there is some dignity in obedience
to my natural self, yielding to the hard-rock miner,
dirty and musky from time spent digging
for solid matter and pointed thoughts,
true as stone cut from the quarry on Marble Mountain.

I think from there the fiercest loose-leaf winds
blow hardest down the North face and across
the open bottomland; time and death both
are quickened, faster than a speeding bullet.

Whatchagot Cookin'?

Not much, these days.
I mean, what day is it anyway?
Thursday? Friday? Hell, it could be
last Monday or next Tuesday today.
There's no way to be sure. These days
the calendar is made of parchment—
weeks and months slide right off. These days
the menu never changes.
Need to stir the pot, I guess.
Whip up a little trouble
just to beat the blanched
unsavory days of doldrum mush.
Once in a measureless while,
a yeasty idea will start to rise
and I knead it, fold it over,
let it rest, punch it down.
It rises again, half-way there—
but turns out on the board
too tough to shape
into a decent loaf
or crusty round. These days
I'll reheat some left-over lines
from the back of the fridge,
maybe spice them up a bit,
make it hot, let the scald
overwhelm good taste
and meaning. These days
whatchagot is whatchaget.

Holy Solstice

Trees shoo the night clouds
and open a dark window
lit by bright starlight.

The Great Conjunction—
high above the swaying trees
two planets unite.

Awash in stardust
the frosted trees, ever green,
bathe in rarest light.

It will shine again
in a winter far beyond
our lives here on Earth.

What eyes will then turn?
What hearts ache for Bethlehem
and trees under stars?

From one tree three owls take flight
on this brightest holy night.

Will Life Return in Spring?

We cast our weary, cloudy eyes toward April
In hopes that the life we once knew is
Like the irrepressible cycle of greening renewal. The
Long-endured misery nurtured by the cruellest

Lack of human decency ends. In the blooming month,
In the crux of Spring—sparrows madly breeding,
Fledglings in sparse feathers fall among the lilacs—
Evergreen hope is not nearly enough. Our way out

Runs in snaking curves against eroding banks of
Easily swollen, flashy creeks, and the
Turmoil of historic floods. Here our Winter dead,
Uncounted, unmourned, foul the awakened land,
Rank in hastily back-hoed graves. Death is mixing
Now with the burgeoning life of April, and memory

Is scattered like seed saved for yesterday and
Never. Be quick to love the ones that you desire.

Sing full-throated and give voice to stirring
Poetry. Lift up your eyes, no matter how dull.
Rise! Rise though grounded by quarantined roots.
Into tomorrow we survivors all go, armed with
Natural prayers and give anxious welcome to Spring.
Give thanks to be washed in a warm April rain.

April, Year Two

It's April yet we're due to get some snow
and colder valley nights. I'm ready for
the warmer days that lie ahead. I know
we need this rain. We need the sky to pour.

So long and dark, this winter left us frail
as grimmer news we heard at every turn.
We hope tomorrow tells a better tale,
hope this summer forests will not burn.

It's hard to even draw a decent breath
or find a way to measure all we've lost.
For a year our lives were wrapped in death.
We can't begin to gauge the human cost.

Our sight is blurred; our nerves are worn.
New storms blow in while still we mourn.

What the world needs now is

Love, sweet love, for sure,
but also a big old steaming heap
of Abracadabra to set things straight.
A world as messed up as this one
we've made won't be fixed
by politicians and sycophants,
or by the squeaky wheels
with the biggest cans of oil.
We need Magicians, scores of them,
with more than rabbits in their hats.
And bring on the Wizards, too,
with big-ass wands and sparkly robes.
We need a full Coven of Witches
with powerful spells, I tell you!
Come on, Weird Sisters,
boil and bubble will barely touch
this toil and trouble, This right here
is a steaming mean shit-storm.
We need mad potions!
Heat up the cauldron
and brew something up.
Turn a murder of crows into
a passel of Priests in black robes
to exorcise these demons
of ignorance and ineptitude
now bringing us down.
Turn loose the Poets!
Turn loose the Poets!
Pour each an eight-count
of hocus-pocus spirits, make it neat,
and we'll give the world
what the world needs now.

The year that wasn't was

longer than any year, ever
even though time blurred and smeared
one gray day into the next,
week after smudged week
and month after foggy month.
How did it get to be Friday already?
The month is half gone
and it just started! How is it
we don't know
where the time has gone?
How can something fly by
at a warped speed
and yet go on forever?

The year that wasn't was
also fuller than any year ever,
even though our homes were
mostly empty and often silent,
except for lovely sounds
of sparrows and larks
and other favorite singers;
except for irresistible scents
of bread baking, soups simmering,
freshly cut bunches of oregano and thyme
tied and drying in the harvest room.

Our lives so abruptly scaled down,
stripped to bare bones
and unceremoniously cancelled,
became simply more beautiful,
as we learned to be
frugal, resourceful and self-sufficient
so we could be
more generous and more giving
for our communities;

more patient and more kind
for our neighbors;
more loving and more thankful
for our families and friends;
and more grateful
for the timeless blue-sky days
now peeping over the horizon.

II

Diana Coogle

Poet's statement:

2020, that year of grief and difficulty around the world, brought a crushing personal grief to me as well by my husband's unexpected death from cancer. In the interstices of caring and loving, I scrambled each day through the April of his dying to keep my commitment to a poem a day. Was the poetry keeping me sane during that insane time? Or was it simply another part of that insane time—writing through the pandemic, writing through the fires, writing through the agony of my husband's death and the hollow days and nights and weeks that followed? After the poem-a-day of April, after Mike's death on May 6, after the driving necessity of writing from such deep emotion, the Applegate Poets' prompts gradually brought a return to an equilibrium of emotions, when I could look at other topics, pay attention to the world around me, take solace and delight in nature, find humor in life, and let the reality of my husband's death steal more softly into my poetry. The selections here hint at that movement, from the agony of April 2020 to a renewed life by the time April 2021 came to an end.

To T. S. Eliot on the First Day of April, 2020

You're durn tootin', Mr. Eliot,
that *April is the cruelest month*—
this year, certainly, when
fear is in every handful of dust
and we latch onto the word of every *Madame
Sosostris* whose
clairvoyance shows *crowds of people walking round in a
ring,*
eating in restaurants, enjoying theater,
playing music in the same room where we can
hear each other without headphones
pleasures we miss this April
when we say, washing our hands, donning our masks,
restraining the urge to rub eyes and scratch noses,
waving to each other from a six-foot distance,
"*One must be so careful these days*";
when the *unreal city* is every city
with its ghost streets and its silences which,
in those unreal cities in Europe,
are broken every Wednesday night
with applause from balconies for nurses and doctors,
for grocery store clerks, postal carriers, and gas station
attendants.

None of us had thought death would undo so many.

Our *nerves are bad at night*
frazzled from hours in front of the computer
reading books online, playing games
efforts to keep the kids occupied
our bodies ache for a walk in the parks that are closed
the rubber band of our psyches stretches thin as

April stretches before us
cruel in its unwillingness to promise a date
when we can leave behind the *withered stumps of time,*
told upon the walls of our homes, in which we shelter,
longing to know when we can emerge with the *lilacs out of*
          the dead land
and regain spring in our step.

Hurry up, please, it's time.
Hurry up, please, it's time.

To My Husband as He Lies Dying

When birds last sing from springtime boughs, and clouds
Will block the sun of smiles, and kisses fail
To kisses speak; when rain descends like nails
And thund'rous grief enthreats to burst aloud

when now my sheets abrade and scratch like shrouds
And dreams of sweetness, past, implode on waking,
And present touch is sorrow in the making,
all pleasures are by looming heartbreak cowed.

Oh, dear, dear husband mine, now pinned in bed
Fastened tight, by cancer's plague laid prone,
I watch death steal your flesh and blood and bone
And weep to see your body's strength so shed.

Yet still your spirit bathes us all with light
Your voice, your eyes, your thanks speak love tonight.

Living Zen

Before enlightenment, chopping wood and hauling water.
After enlightenment, chopping wood and hauling water.

I went and got my Ph.D. before
I was seventy, and then with that intellectual enlightenment
I came home again and found myself chopping
Vegetables for dinner and hauling wood
For the fire to warm the house and
Wondered what difference it made, all that hauling
Of books and stimulating the mind with ancient water.

Then I got married, after
I was seventy, and lived the enlightenment
Of love until cancer came chopping
Down my beloved liked a piece of wood
For the funeral pyre and
Left me hauling
My emptiness around like a bucket of water.

If for a Moment I Could Become

If for a moment I could become
the root that loves the rain
maybe I would water my garden more carefully.

If I could become
the blossom that loves the bee,
the nut that loves the bird,
the dirt that loves the worm,
maybe I would love more assiduously my garden soil.

If I could become
the air that sings to the hummingbird's wing
and swings the spider's thread like a hammock,
I know I would try harder at my pranayama.

If I could become
the rainbow that arcs like a mother's arm
when the sun drops a kiss on the rain's new face,
I would more often drop colors on the black days of others.

If for a moment I could become
the wave that carries the whale's song,
the silence that crackles when the frost goes hard
the dark that lights the Milky Way's path,
maybe then I would know at last
that I am not picked out by myself
but am hitched by deep nerve patterns
to everything else in the Universe.

A Litany for the Craftsperson

Oh, carpenter, who built my house
Oh, chef, who pleases my palate
Oh, baker, whose bread is broken with thanks
Oh, vintner, whose wine has nose and legs, with a touch on
the tongue that sings of oak
Oh, glassblower, whose glass has a smooth oops of fallibility
against my lip
Oh, welder, who crafted water, sky, and mountain in iron for
my staircase
Oh, potter, wielder of the wheel that whorls the clay into
cups and plates
Oh, woodworker, whose lathe-turned bowls hold salads and
rose petals and my husband's ashes
Oh, toymaker, whose trains entrance the children
Oh, dollmaker, too, for puppets of magic and play-acting
dolls
Oh, weaver of rugs
Oh, maker of soap and candles and brooms
Oh, seamstress, who makes clothes and pillows, curtains
and coats
Oh, knitter of socks and pull-over-the-ears hats for snow
Oh, bookmaker for my handmade journal
Oh, bootmaker for the softest leather shoes
Oh, basket maker
Oh, furniture maker
Oh, flower arranger, with a conjurer's touch
Oh, calligrapher, whose letters speak meaning by their look
on the page
Oh, landscaper, a wizard with the placement of plants
Oh, lavender crafter for wreaths and sachets
Oh, stained-glass artist for sunbursts of color
Oh, master gardener
Oh, master brewer
Oh, master photographer

Oh, sculptor
Oh, painter
Oh, poet.
You who work with your hands and your heart
you who bring joy and warmth to our lives with your craft
you who know the value of work well done
    a tool well kept
    time slowed to the speed of hands in this day of manufactured everything
        of ready-made clothes and go-to-the-store to buy your shoes
        of cheap goods at the Dollar Store and meals in a packet to heat up and serve
you who know the meditative space 'twixt hand and tool
you who weave love into your wares
    hammer or sew or weld it in
    plant or cook or ferment it in—
you do more than tie us with nostalgic ribbons to the perfect past.
You remind us to bring our hands and our hearts
to the tender present.

Bobby Adams

Bobby Adams, third-grade crush
Those short blond curls, that blue-eyed gaze
A laugh that turned my heart to mush
So smart he earned Miss Pfeiffer's praise.

Bobby Adams, third-grade king
But spin-the-bottle gave me Leon
I took that kiss but felt the sting
'Twas not the king's but lowly peon's.

Bobby Adams, now where are you?
And who? And what have you become?
Banker? Chef? Philanderer untrue?
Philanthropist with ungodly sum?

Bobby Adams, a hippy dude?
Blond curls caught in ponytail,
Smoke a pipe and swim all nude,
Beat a drum and eat raw kale?

Bobby Adams, unknown part.
But one thing is my fervent hope:
That I did not give my third-grade heart
To one who's now a Trumpist dope.

Message in a Bottle

To whoever picks up this bottle
which I have cast into the ocean at the coast of Oregon:
you who might have picked it up
from a beach just under the Brooks Range in Alaska
where you are vacationing from your vineyard, just inland.
Or maybe you reached out of what was once a fourteenth-
floor window
and picked up this bottle from one of the inlets flowing
between buildings
that are now the streets of San Francisco cum Venice.
I write because I want you to know
that once there were wolves in the Oregon hills
and whales in the deeps of our oceans.
Those tales you've heard are true.
I myself have seen elephants and giraffes
And swum with giant whale sharks.
I have heard birds sing like symphonies
and have known people who have seen
Monarch butterflies in mass migration.
I am sorry you will never experience these miracles.
I knew frogs at the time of their disappearance.
You cannot imagine the magic of frogs.
I am writing to tell you
that snow is not a myth
that it is softer, whiter, more pure
than your imagination can conceive.
I write because I want you to know
how beautiful the world was before
and to tell you to be careful with what you have
not only not to lose what is left of that once gorgeous world
but also because if you are careful now
and if you learn from our mistakes
maybe, slowly, that greater world
will revive.

Ode to a Winter Landscape

Nothing is so beautiful as a winter landscape
When fire-folks of frost in the frozen fields
wink rainbows at the morning sun
When the unity of white undoes dappled things
When the squeak of skis on snow
sneaks into the unity of silence
in the snow-muffled forest
When the air is so cold it hurts your teeth to smile
But you can't
stop
smiling
Because nothing is so beautiful
As snow-laden fir boughs against a cobalt sky
the descending blue rushing towards whipped-cream
peaks
Nothing is so beautiful as the kiss of snowflakes
whisper-soft from steel-gray clouds
Nothing more magical than the inaudible fall
of snow outside the window
descending like down from overstuffed clouds
as the fire in the stove at your back shines like shook
foil
Nothing is so beautiful as winter stars
splintering in the cold air
of a landscape which—
winter scene
sweet, especial winter scene—
is charged with grandeur
and
gathers to a greatness
of insuperable cold
unsurpassable silence
unconditional beauty

Walk with Me the Stein Butte Trail

It begins rough so you have to be
tough enough to handle stuff like
rocky ground at first, and then
burst after burst of good long climbs.
You have to be sound of body and strong of mind
and let your feet do the steep
so you can keep your eye on the sky-reaching firs
of the deep shaded forest on the steep inclines
and be alert to find, without passing it,
the canyon live oak whose roots cloak the rock
with barely a crack for an acorn's lodging;
so you can greet in passing the grove of madrones,
sleek and lithe as dancers, and the diva
whose double trunks leap with balletic grace.
It's not a race, so slow your pace to amaze your soul
at the Grandfather oak, so old and still holding
its massive limbs boldly on the forest-dark slope;
and again at six hard-boned, red-toned madrone
trunks bowing heads over a basal pool of cool rainwater
like monks in prayer at a baptismal font;
and again at ferns that droop in loop-de-loops
from a moss-faced group of tucked-in boulders.
In autumn, a gulch of gold-plundered maples.
In winter snow-capes draped on mountains' shoulders.
In spring a trove of broken rainbows
where wildflowers grow on open slopes.

After more than an hour of breath-stealing pull
the body deals easily with a ridgetop stroll
where a view of the Siskiyou Crest
arrests your steps and suggests a prayer
or a praise, a gape or a gaze
before you raise a salute and make
your way again towards the butte till

the trail ups the ante and asks for plenty,
pitches wickedly up again,
and makes immersion in exertion what it takes
to trick the body into kicking on up.

Another hour and a quarter, and exertion peaks
at the last and steepest, calf-cringing creep
up the steep rocky point of the Butte itself
with the mind reminding that the Little Engine could
and the body refinding what it would
do to put you atop the butte,
where the fluttering flute of your breath finds calm
in the balm of solitude renewed and mountains viewed
on all sides 'round—the Siskiyou Crest, the region's crown,
to the west, and to the east, a streak of Cascade peaks
over the placid blue of Applegate Lake.
In a twinkle of sun on the summit's brink
I think you'll find a pink-lipped Lewisia,
and with that link to Paradisia,
drink in the wine imbibed from the Stein Butte climb:
beauty large and beauty small
soul fulfillment from body's all.

On the Second Movement of Mozart's Clarinet Concerto

Oh, how can music be at once so sad
and beautiful? For mountain scenes do not
cause mournful tears, and when the sun explodes
cathedral gloom with stained-glass light, my soul
weeps not but fills with love and beauty's balm.
But at the first six notes, adagio,
of clarinet's lament in Mozart's piece,
tears fill my eyes and drop on folded hands
as clarinet descends to gut-wrenched depths,
then tip-toes slowly to the airy dome
of open sky beyond our ken, so light
I barely see its sound, as like a hawk
it climbs and gyres to heaven's lofty sphere.
These solitary notes are heart-break true,
for hearts that break will always break alone.
Then like a tragic choir of ancient Greece
the orchestra swells up to reassure:
"We understand; we've been there, too. Your grief
is ours." My soul leans into music's grace
that lifts my heart and stills my mind, the notes
so delicate, so deep, so much like life:
so beautiful, so sad, so full, so sweet.

III

Beate Foit

Poet's Statement:

At a time when life has almost returned to normal, it feels strange to reflect on my memories and feelings during the COVID-19 pandemic that began 16 months ago.

Everything came to an abrupt halt in March 2020. The life to which we were accustomed ceased to exist. No choir or theater performances, no celebrations with family or friends, no human touch outside our homes.

It felt surreal. We had to adjust to this new normal: weekly poems shared online instead of once a month in person. Here we could encourage each other through this dark period of time in our lives. We held the space for each other as we learned to live through the pandemic.

Numb, angry, and sad, a world without shared laughter but frequent worries, a volatile political climate, severe wildfires killing people, decimating old growth forests and vibrant communities.

Initially, we hoped to "return to normal" by last summer, yet rapidly increasing numbers of infected and dying people painted a grim picture. By September, we had accepted the fact that this pandemic would last well into the new year, and it did.

Focusing on poetry helped me to describe my inner and outer world.

Spring Restoration

The big garden awaits.
Two apple trees in full bloom
and in between a wilderness;
a microcosmos that lives between the weeds.

Two apple trees in full, soft-pink bloom.
They were pruned not too long ago.
A wild microcosmos covered by weeds
will disappear when the soil is tilled.

The strong branches will bear fruit
while ants, snails, beetles, spiders
will disappear when the beds are tilled
for the fallow soil is ready now.

Ants, snails, beetles, spiders -
there is a wilderness in between seasons.
The fallow soil is ready now,
and the big garden awaits.

Half a Century

Are we at crossroads again
just like in 1970 when
a massive oil spill in
Santa Barbara
birthed the idea
of celebrating Earth Day?

We had only an inkling then
about the devastating effects
that our mistreatment of this planet
would have on future generations
who rightfully blame us elders
who should have been wiser.

Humanity still drives pick up trucks
and uses plastic wrappings,
perhaps more with a guilty
conscience now than before-
but still, we continue the destruction;
icebergs are melting, sea levels rising.

Coronavirus with all its ill side effects
has one benefit -
it allows the earth to heal slowly
because we are limited
in our movements,
in our consumption.

Let's hope we won't forget this:
clean air, blue skies,
mountains hidden for decades
are visible now,
wild animals in our front yards,
friends reaching out to us.

Mirrored by the River

1
Early morning walk
Sweet blackberries melt on tongue
Sun rising up red

2
River flows quietly
Blue heron spreads wings rising
Queen Anne's Lace blooming

3
Crisp air hints at fall
Otter floats and plays in reeds
Excited dog barks

4
Forest animals
Blend with fallen Madrone leaves
Once green moss turned brown

5
Deep-red setting sun
Solitary river walk
Blue Heron feeds its offspring

~

Mountains mirrored by the river at night
in meteor showers' shimmering light.

The Moldau

I am water
Hiding in the ground
bubbling and swelling
I push through loose soil
I am a spring

I tumble over rocks
through grasses
dragonflies dance upon me
wildlife drinks from me
I am a nourisher

My path widens
snow melts and converges
infuses me with clear water again
I am stronger now and push over banks
I flood pastures

Soon I am wider
than I could have dreamt becoming
the current increases
small boats sail on my surface
waves trail their sterns
the water calms as evening descends

In my silvery dress, under a crescent moon
I am gliding past cities and villages
their lights glitter on my waves
fish skip to the surface and dive down again
evading the fishers' nets

Industries release their toxic waste
their gullies empty into me
fish die
no more children playing giddily
along my bank

I crave to empty into the vast ocean
crave the clean waters of my spring
I know I cannot turn back the tide
cannot return to my place of birth
I am bemoaning what I have become

My wish is to seek shelter
in the tiny subterraneous trickle
I once was
to disappear into safety
rather than being what I am now

Fires

The fires around us
are vicious,
unforgiving,
scarring.

When the devastation hits home,
and friends watch their houses
go up in flames,
bereft of possessions,
the only thing left are memories
of what once was their life.

When flames shoot sky high
and whole forests are decimated
and ashes dance in the fire storm,
you ask yourself, "What is essential?"
as you prepare to leave
at a moment's notice.

You pack up your life
into a few boxes,
knowing full well
your heart will break
should what's left behind
become part of the fire.

There is so much sorrow,
so much loss.
This heavy energy concentrates
in the sepia-colored smoke
that settles in and suffocates the valleys.

Once beautiful trees,
along with our lungs,
are struggling for breath,
for air, for clear skies,
for survival.

You are waiting for rain,
to wash away
the layers of soot, of ashes,
of tears and anger,
to have a clean slate
for a fresh start.

Is emptiness the bandage
that will heal the numbness?
Will it help to protect
against more assaults
will it help to protect
fire-sour emotions?

When is enough - ENOUGH?

Thanksgiving

This year's unsurmountable sadness,
visits with loved ones are on hold.
The hope that this pandemic
will vanish in thin air
is an illusion.
Promises, cures,
a vaccine?
Maybe
soon.

Hope that the lockdown is lifted soon,
that absence will reduce sickness.
Loved ones - no hug, no embrace,
hoping that a vaccine
further reduces
outbreak worldwide.
Let's be strong,
each one!
Wait!

A Hygge Recipe

December arrives,
greyness settles in.
Shorter days
with tea at 4.

Turn on the water,
fill the teapot
with Chinese Pu Erh.
Steam's rising visibly.

Let it steep quietly.
Take two biscuits
from the Italian tin,
put them on a porcelain plate.

Place near the green wreath
where the center white candle is aglow,
casting shadows on the wall.

Roses painted on the body
of a porcelain cup,
transparent against the candle light.
The tea seems to evaporate

with every sip.
It's fragrance lingers.
I feel warm
inside and out

with a fire in the wood stove
with the dog curled around
my feet under the table.
Danish comfort.

Current Times

The wait is over. Inauguration Day finally came.
The insurrection and its aftermath will never be erased.
Many firsts within the White House. Breathing will become
less strained.

Not quite an Ode to Spring

Second covid spring. I'm yearning for sun.
Frogs serenade from a neighbor's pond.
Their company welcome, their chorus fun.

Tulips, daffodils, and tender fern frond;
yellow and white crocuses dance a *ronde*,
brightly dotting the slowly greening grass.

I bid Winter *Adieu*, Spring's back, sweet lass!
Stressed soil enriched with last year's dark compost,
witch hazel and daphne cut back, *en masse*,
produce fragrant blossoms - I love the most.

Musings

It seems like
we are surrounded
by deep darkness
sparkled with stars.

They are no longer
the sole inhabitants
of a universe detached
yet connected.

It is frightening
to imagine
that our planet
is suspended,

a globe
in a system
of galaxies
born by chance.

Sometimes
when I feel lost,
cut off from the world,
I dream about the similarities

that connect us,
marvel about the light
we are seeing
from stars long extinguished.

Will it happen to earth?
Will its light shine
on others
long after it ceased to exist?

IV

Seth Kaplan

Poet's Statement:

I was not writing before the pandemic. I was busy. My busy was expressed in good deeds, hard work, building something. Good, lots of good. It was as if I was a perpetual motion train, building my own track to keep going. Pandemic didn't exactly change that. If anything, it created more fuel, more desire to do more. But as the months went by, friends from a long past began to reach out, and one of those dear friends was poetry. We started by catching up, sharing family stories, memories. And soon, as we remembered ourselves and the trust we had earned through the years, we began to ask, "But, really, how *are* you? This pandemic has really been something. Is anything different?" My pandemic poems can seem random. While I tried writing specifically about the pandemic, I never created anything I thought worth sharing. I realize now I wrote not of an event but of a journey. The poems shared herein express my experiences from living through a time that changed us all in intimate ways, from a distance.

Memories of Good Times to Come
--for my father

We would be friends
you and I
if not for the inconvenience
of death.

But what is death
if not the giving of oneself
to something new?
As in life unto death.

And, so, today,
on this anniversary of you
no longer, I see you, finally-
inconvenience is no matter.

I come to this joining carrying my shame before me
for my practice of social distancing
long before we had those words.
Your love was so much and I was so small.

Let us walk together
on this land you never knew
except in your dreams.
Dream with me today

And you can call out
the names of things
as the wind caresses
and soothes the ancestral wounds.

Let us embrace across generations as brothers.
Let me know there is redemption
from the years of missing you,
mistaking gentleness for weakness.
I miss you now.

Let us walk together, you and I,
and let us rename all those things
we thought we knew.
Let us rejoice in the memories
of good times to come.

Untitled & Unfinished

Why do I have no words for you?
You who fed me words
I took as nourishment.
So many words,
yours and mine,
though mine emerged silent
but for scratches on a page.
Why speak of wounds scabbed over now?
Neither shedding blood, nor light,
nor answers.
Each only the geological layers
from which molehills form mountains.

You taught me to worship words
each one sacred, precious, searing, unforgiving.
You taught me story is all
powerful, greater than truth.
You taught me love is currency
a metaphor for uncertainty
a simile for need
rhyming with chaos.
Words, story, truth, love.
Written and erased on an etch-a-sketch
and only through exercise and time
are the scars revealed.

I have taken all you taught me
and I find myself searching,
still, for the words
that will tell the story.
Words to wipe the slate clean.
Words to bring clarity.

Over and over the words rearrange.
The stories change, truth eludes.
Love, the echo of a distant call
in the borderlands
between light and dark.
And it is there I begin again
to find you
to find us
to find me.

Naming Stars

I do not know
the names of the stars
I struggle
with names generally
and naming stars can seem
like naming grains of sand
or snowflakes
or heartbeats
But that is not it
I look to the stars
and see mystery
and I do not seek a name

I did name a star once
My Grandma Anna
saw wonder in everything
A peasant daughter
among siblings too many
to track, she came to America
as a teenager
with her Zionist husband
and created a new way
Rejoicing in every challenge
Ever hopeful
Her stories never ended
with what is
but with what might yet be

And so, near the end
of her life,
I named a star for her
And when I shared

the certificate showing her name,
and a personalized message
from the Star Registry,
her eyes opened big as the moon
and wet as the dawn
I did not know such a thing was possible
she said, as she looked at me
with wonder

There are more stars
than we have numbers
and I know the name of one
Anna is up there,
amongst so many others,
shedding her light
over the world's darkness.

Fear

What do you fear
that you have not already materialized
in your conjurer mind?
Shaped by forces
you know too well
Visions from funhouse mirrors
are not all you face
While you furtively crochet
loopholes in your reasoning,
so much more awaits your attention

What is this suffocating fear
you cling to like a final breath?
Only sticks and stones
bricks and bones, fanciful walls
designed to keep your what-ifs at bay
lest they transform
into something that guides you
to those unvisited places
What waits for you
in the rooms of your life?

What has fear to show you
that you have not already discovered?
Embrace the lessons you have set aside
Your senses are attuned to these moments
Caressing the contours
of what you mistakenly call the unknown
As if you are not
the creator of this world
Fearful of your brilliance.
and the choices awaiting.

Ides of April

If you step outside
as the light is being born
on the Ides of April
the spirits will speak

If you walk in silence and with purpose
the trees will whisper ancient stories
from the beginning
when humans knew the magic

If you explore with the eyes of your soul
and the ears of your heart
the wizards and witches in your fields
will show themselves and greet you

If you step into the raging wind
you will learn the source of its anger
and raise your arms and howl
like the animal you are

Star Thistle

Who is Star Thistle
in this time
populated by people of strong beliefs
lining roads and sidewalks
like feudal armies,
banners emblazoned,
shouting your shame
celebrating their goodness

Where I live, we gather
in fields and living rooms
to decry the invasion
of Star Thistle
We make pointed remarks
condemning Star Thistle spikes
for piercing soles and ankles
Dangerous to our more gentle kinds
Non-native, unwelcome
They don't belong

Star Thistle arrives
when all else is lost
In the desert season
when the verdant coat
of our craggy land
turns to straw and dust
Star Thistle flourishes
when others call it quits

I walk in a field of Star Thistle
most days these days
But this day it is new, less threatening

Yellow blooms shining like lemon drops
And first one bee and then others
swarm those lemon drops of nectar
It figures bees would be the ones
to make friends of Star Thistle
Another condemned for its sting

I make no friend of Star Thistle
nor of bees
But, today, neither do I shout slogans
to their demise
Today, I walk more quietly
through this field
Knowing how much I miss
And how much I misunderstand

American Dream

What's it worth?
Showing up, day after day,
to move the gizmos built by some poor son of a bitch
from some place I can't name
who was unfortunate enough to be born somewhere not
called America.
That guy makes the pieces for pennies I inspect for nine
dollars an hour.
God Bless America. Sends them in a boat the size of a
football stadium
across the ocean so I can inspect them for Americans.
Nine dollars an hour, 60 hours a week, if business is good.
Thirty hours a week when it's not.
When business is good, I pay my rent.
When it's not, the bills clutter from the kitchen into the living
room.
Business ain't been good for a while
so I'm stacking the bills neatly from the confusion of my
living room
to a corner of the kitchen.
I need to clear the sofa for Davey. We decided
to make ends meet by becoming roomies.
I'm stacking the bills into neat piles like rows of houses.
Makes me think
how I wanted to own a house, mow a lawn,
wash a car in the driveway and wave at my neighbors.
I'll be able to wave at Davey from the kitchen.
We'll look at each other over a cup of coffee and wonder
what's it worth?
But mostly we'll keep our eyes to ourselves, thinking
that poor son of a bitch.
Thank God at least I ain't come to that.

Shanah Tovah

Shanah Tovah
Peace be with you
No promise of a good year
has been made to you
Only the promise
you make to yourself
affirm to others
and the manner in which you honor it

Shanah Tovah
Peace be with you
Today you cry for lost and wounded mothers
The mother of conscience
mother creator, mother earth
The one who birthed you
Battered and bloodied all
But the feminine is fierce
and will not relent
Calling like a shofar
Shanah Tovah
Peace be with you
As her just voice gives out finally
She does not ask you to rise in defense, only
to stand beside and join in the fight

Shanah Tovah
Peace be with you
Stand at the well and reflect
You waver and radiate, dumbstruck
by your own image
But the well is not glass
It does not resist or shatter
It is your kindred
Wishing you well

It draws you in
Depth masked by stillness

Shanah Tovah
Peace be with you
Who dares this immersion?
How many before you
have tossed coins and marveled
at the shiny glow?
Do not cast for dreams
Do not skuttle across the surface
like a water bug
thinking this is your world
Trust your animal senses
Dive in
Do not trust your eyes
Dive in
Do not hold your breath
Drink up

Poet's note: Shanah Tovah means "good year" and is the traditional greeting on Rosh Hashanah, the Jewish new year. Shofar is a ram's horn blown to signify important messages.

Stillness

Raven, winged messenger
soaring on the breath of the canyon
Your home is the wind
not quite heaven
not quite earth
filling the void
Soaring in the stillness
of this ancient world
Speaking the words
of an ancient language
in the rhythm of your wings

Across the valley
Boulder sits, watching
in silence, teaching
me to see
through patient knowing
A learned Buddha
carved through centuries in stillness
always in stillness
is vision born
and wisdom revealed

Seek stillness
though your heart beats
wild and erratic
Know stillness
Let the river carry
the debris of your thinking away
Let the wind soften your edges
Feel gravity draw you in
closer to your home
Plant your feet on the earth
rooted and nourished

There Is A Gate

There is a gate
The gate locks shut
The gate swings freely both ways
It is a gate
And it offers no clue
To the shape of your soul
It is only you and only yours
To decide if this gate is to guard
Or to step through

There is a gate
You stand on one side
Day after day and wonder
Which side of the gate is this?
Is it the side of the oppressed?
Or the oppressor?
Are you defending this gate?
Or trying to break through?
Should you open this gate graciously?
Or hold it fast with the last breath of your life?

There is a gate
And just now you hear voices
Disembodied shouts and whispers
Pleas to save the gate
To give your life to the gate
And there is silence and space
Where you question
The very existence of this gate

There is a gate
And there
And there
There is a gate

V

H. Ní Aódagaín

Poet's Statement:

Why write, when the sky is falling?
What to say, when the end of the world seems imminent?
How to form lines of a poem, when a plague is rampaging,
its reach extending to the ends of the earth?

Can words ever be a salve for the losses our families, our nation, our global community have suffered in this pandemic, the tragedy we have endured? Though we as a group of poets didn't set out to answer that question, the task of showing up, putting pen to paper and responding to the call gave voice to our silent tears, allowed space to grieve, and encouraged us to honor life in the midst of incomprehensible death.

The following poems reveal the different moods the group's prompts elicited in me. From rage to rejoicing; from reflecting on the past to imagining the face of the future; from fighting despair to seeking beauty in the heart of a flower. In order to write poetry in this unprecedented time, I had to be still and notice, be present to what was right in front of me, to understand that the only moment is *now*. My hope is that these poems will offer others a similar solace.

Spring's Return

The rosemary opens to blue
peonies stand regal, their stalks
magenta against swaths of newly green
veronica, planted for my mother,
purples the garden's edge.

As April arrives, I should only know joy,
life returning after winter's fallow,
promise of earth's abundance.

Instead, grief—joy's opposite
hobbles my heart
stuns my breath.

I grieve as thousands die
in villages, towns, and cities
across this spinning Earth
no borders able to hold back
this unrelenting march of death.

I grieve the grandmother
whose last breath was heard
by no one,
the doctor who died for
having healed another.

I grieve the families huddled
in tents, refugees of war,
fearing what is coming,
what more they must endure.

I grieve
the dreams upended
the futures vanished
the hope stilled.

Yet, amid this sorrow, the garden beckons.
Rows of fertile earth call to be seeded,
wish to produce their rightful bounty.
Budding trees color the skies,
boughs of pink and white herald
the summer's fruit, autumn's harvest.

Within the cycle of life, death.
Within the cycle of death, life.

Grief and Joy, Joy and Grief
the Yin and Yang of now.

I am Enraged

Enraged — to be propelled by rage
Enrage — to act so that another rises in fury against you
Rage — anger, uncontrolled, accompanied by violent
screaming or—more dangerous—a fierce
burning sitting in the pit of your stomach
building, gathering strength with each new
revelation

of how evil they really are.

Enraged, I am enraged

that three-year-old children
torn from their mothers
now lie on concrete floors,
scared, sick, suffering

Enraged, I am enraged

by millionaires bickering
should our workers receive
$1200 or $1500, a one-time payment
to help "shore up the economy"
while $350 *billion* is stuffed into suitcases
handed out to "struggling" CEOs

Enraged, I am enraged

each time this country's "president"
opens his mouth and his diseased words,
like the virus that threatens to destroy us,
fall in droplets onto his sycophants,
and they, doomed by their delusional devotion,
lap them up like manna

Enraged, I am enraged

that in NYC on Friday, April 3rd, in the year 2020
people are dying, one person every ten minutes
falling like flies, stacked in refrigerated trucks,
hospitals running out of every supply they need,
including the bags to hold the bodies.

Where will our mass graves be dug?

Walking the Talk

Sometimes I want to *do* less and *be* more.
I worry too much, too often
I fail to practice what I know
the answer to all dilemma

Breath in, breath out

A pandemic has struck, global in scope
the worst feared has become true, nothing
will be as before,
but what hasn't changed:
I am still here with these thoughts
that only I can silence

Breath in, breath out

**** ****

If there were no tomorrow,
I'd start the day with a crystal flute
of cold champagne, sip it slowly as
I watch the first light of morning
wake from its dreaming

I'd turn on Vivaldi to full volume
and aim it at the mountain tops
so the valley would be filled with music

I'd sit in the garden long enough to witness
the first shoots emerging from the dark earth
the unfurling of a spinach leaf,
the reaching of a pea tendril toward its trellis

**** ****

My wild, wry, wicked friend
Liza died last week
I sat at her feet, anticipating

her last breath

Time ticked by on the bedside clock
but in that room,
as she labored to be released,
there was only

breath in, breath out

until there wasn't.

**** ****

Can I permit myself
to just *sit*
for as long as necessary
till I become only

breath in, breath out

and the illusion of a finite life merges
with the reality of the infinite?

In Homage to the Old Ones

When I walk in woods where the old ones remain:
the great Madrones, Doug Firs, Sugar Pines,
my eyes rise up to where
their tips touch the sky, where
their crowns join with cloud

The old ones
not taken by man and his machines—
the chain saws, feller bunchers, robotic arms—
stand resistant to Greybeard, rust beetle, drought
solitary amid younger forest inhabitants.

Humbled at their feet, I pray.
"Please stay with us. By your existence,
I recalibrate time, relinquish selfishness,
and remember when we walked
under you in reverence."

Ironic, just as we humans have begun to honor
the intelligence contained in a community of trees,
the unseen networks below the forest floor,
the interdependence of all beings everywhere,
we gather on the precipice,
looking into a futureless moment.

When I walk in woods that hold the old ones,
my eyes rise and I pray.

This is a Time of Sorrow

This is a time of sorrow—

sorrow that speaks in the absence of words

sorrow that weeps after all tears have fallen

sorrow that presses down, like mid-July heat
when spring breezes have ceased to soften the air

sorrow that circles, closer and closer, like an osprey
in search of the silver glint of fish

sorrow that sits at the edge of every breath

sorrow that lodges itself in the bone's marrow
in the corpuscles of blood coursing through our bodies

sorrow that turns the stomach,
like spoiled milk, like poisoned water

sorrow that silences the heart
drapes it in shroud cloth so no light may enter

sorrow that haunts the soul
no reason or rationale to be found
for the voices one hears,
for the shadows that dance on the wall

sorrow that is deaf to the sound of life's calling
the ringing of joy, the hopeful beating of a pulse

This is a time of sorrow.

We have lost so much.

What If?

What if she hadn't
put on her one good dress, nor
pinned her fine hair to the nape of her neck,
hadn't polished the clunky black shoes, her only pair,
or joined the other maids and governesses
employed by the big houses on the hill
to dance at the Saturday night *Ceílí*
in the basement of St. Joseph's Catholic Church?

The women had come from the old country
lured by the promise of jobs and transport paid,
the ploy of an American bishop
to ensure that the Irish men of his parish
would marry their own kind.

What if she hadn't left that forsaken island
unwilling to face her mother's grief,
to hug her siblings one last time?
What if she hadn't stood at the door
of the two-room cottage, bogs of peat
stretching for miles, and dreamed of more,
her keen intelligence unmet by
the schoolmarm's parochial instruction?

We called her Nana, my mother's mother
only photographs recall her face
I, too little to remember her before
an embolism killed her on the surgeon's table.

"Your grandmother's floors were so clean,
you could eat off them," the only mention
of her in all the years of my childhood.
Was my own mother's grief too much to bear:
her husband, mother, and mother-in-law

each beloved and loved, taken the same year,
her only recourse, silence?

Only much later, many years on
would a remnant surface of my Nana.
In New Jersey to visit Uncle,
her youngest of four, the only remaining,
I journey to the house they grew up in.
A quaint faux Victorian dwarfed by modern
brick homes, I creep through the neighbor's yard
to glimpse the tangled back garden.
A wooden staircase plunges down,
turns once, and then again, to meet the ground.
From the recesses of six decades, the image
of my Nana standing at the top of the stairs,
her sternness spoken by the tight smile she wears.

What if, that long ago Saturday night,
amidst the sounds of fife, fiddle and *bodhran*
she hadn't heard him ask for the next dance,
hadn't turned to see sky blue eyes sparkling
from a handsome face, a smile that
made all her trouble worthwhile?

What if?

A Kaleidoscope World

Late evening email to heal a rupture,
then to bed, where I fall,
like Alice down the rabbit hole,
into a kaleidoscope world
of sign and symbol

Quarreling with the abbess
"You rarely have time for me,"
my estranged brother appears
We fix the windshield of his
rainbow-colored bus, press
silicone to patch the holes.
Are these two people
one and the same?

Why in this dreamscape
am I on the road,
unprepared? Nowhere to sleep
counting on friends
whose rooms are too full.

Why in this dream's plot
must I bring bad news,
"Marianne is dead"
when, in morning's light,
that will not be true?

What I dread
about dreaming:
the things I see that have
yet to occur—
symbol or portent?

The cast of characters I conjure
often those long gone
best friend who betrayed,
cherished mother, now priestess
vivid portraits whose detail astounds

I swim with schools
of outrageous ocean creatures,
stand below majestic mountains
awed at their silent power
I make love that wakes me
with its intensity
I birth babies, and lose them
and find them again
I climb towers, race down empty streets
smash windows, foil assailants
I confront evil
I bow before the Goddess.

Magic, mysterious realities I live
until daylight enters
and whisks away the wonder.

Madrid

Color her warm, chestnut brown
the red of a *rioja* spilling
into my glass, smooth on my tongue

Color her salted, black, green
the olives of her southern climes
pungent flesh giving way to juicy pleasure

Color her soft, golden dusk edging
the tree-lined courtyard
a bookseller talks of Lorca
I come away with leather-bound wonders

Color her mind-blowing, awe-inspiring
hours walking the halls of the Prado
        Fra Angelico's haloed *Annunciation*
        The Three Graces by Rubens
        Breughel's demonic fantasies
there for the viewing
there for the honoring

(Returning late to the hostel, owner turned friend
expresses his concern. "You've been gone since
early morning. I was worried."
In a dreamlike trance, I answer.
"I spent all day at the Prado."
"Oh, oh, yes," he nodds. "I understand.")

Color her sobering, stark
the black and white masterpiece
        Guernica
Picasso's wall-length response
to the horror of modern-day war

Color her open-hearted, sun-splashed
the smiles of the *madrileños*
a people clear in their priorities
afternoons spent at a café table
among family, friends, newcomers
freedom in the present
having endured a dictatorial past

Color her deeply familiar
vaulted walkways,
filigreed balconies of
wrought-iron lace,
terracotta tiled roofs,
flower-draped gardens

decadence and demise
in an ongoing dance

like the city of my childhood
New Orleans
the only other city that
ever stole my heart

An "Aha" moment
when history illuminates

I've returned to the motherland
I've come home.

Autumn Leaves
This is a poem for two voices.

The green of summer turns
gold, orange, red
leaves in splendored array
Harvest celebrations begin

> *Leaves desiccated, brown*
> *fall too early*
> *taken not by the chill of Autumn*
> *but by the drought of summer*
> *the lack of rain winter past*

Pirates, princesses, ninja warriors
swarm front doors
sacks bulge with candy
joyful abundance

> *A plague in our streets*
> *traditions stilled*
> *schools shuttered, kids confined*
> *to screens in isolated living rooms*

The first fires are lit
houses warm as
evening's chill advances

> *Smoke-saturated skies unending*
> *cars packed with life's belongings*
> *people fleeing down mountain roads*
> *as flames lick at the edge of our*
> *nightmares*

Trees relinquish their autumn fruit
cinnamon-laced sauce bubbles
on the stove, enough to store

and more to give away
round tubs of shiny red orbs
Who can grab one with their teeth?

We pray for rain
we pray for respite
we search for some semblance
of our lives as they were

Geese fly south
their calls bisect the sky
urging us to remember
what is to come

But there is only the crushing
silence of the charred forest
the blackened earth

The darkening day
the colder nights
frost on the pumpkins
lying swollen in the fields

The scales have tipped
we wander unmoored
Can we survive this?

All in balance
seasons come round
the seed must fall
to be birthed anew.

The ancient rhythms
still pulse within us
May we return to
honoring their song.

Untitled

Quiet sits beside me. She calms the heart's beating frenzy.
I rest now. Stillness opens a wider door, invites a new path.
This abode offers nothing but emptiness. I have all I need.

VI

Joan Peterson

Poet's Statement:

I moved through the pandemic with relative ease. My great-grandson was born on February 22, 2020, and since his family and I share a household, I had plenty to keep me occupied during the year of isolation. However, I missed the contact with my poet friends and my singing friends. The month of April was poetry month, so some of us began the challenge of writing a poem a day and sending it out to others who were also writing daily poems. After taking a month off, we realized that the poetry exchange was an important part of having contact with friends, so we began a poem a week, exchanging prompts with suggestions of what to write. This went on throughout the year of 2020 and into 2021. It was a wonderful way of keeping in contact with my poet friends and getting to know each other in an even more intimate way. It also kept us writing, which was a perfect source of motivation. I am thankful for our poetry group and thankful that we were able to keep our poems going through the year of isolation.

Shelter in Place

It came from the top
This command to shelter in place
Sounding so military.

But I am ready with
Shooting stars, buttercups
Hounds tongue, indian warrior.

My bunker a hollow tree
Near the pond.
A varied thrush flies by

A banner in the sky
To say, all is well
Here on the planet.

No harm will come
To the wild things.
Our thoughts

Need healing.

The Tree With Lights In It
from Annie Dillard's Pilgrim At Tinker Creek

I saw the tree with lights in it.
each cell buzzing with flame.
Seeing for the first time
grass that was wholly fire
knocked breathless by a powerful glance.

Gradually the lights went out
cells un-flamed and disappeared.
I was still ringing. I had been a bell
my whole life and never knew it until
at that moment I was lifted and struck.

I have very rarely seen the tree
with the lights in it, but I live for it,
for the moment a new light roars
through the crack, and the mountains slam.

Groundhog Day

When Punxsutawney Phil crawls
out of his den, no shadow appears.
We know six weeks of winter is ahead.
That suits me fine. I love to walk along
the creek in winter, watching the water tumble
over logs, hearing the sound of waterfalls,
rocks pushing their way through the stream.

In summer the creek is dry. Bears
use it for their trail through the woods.
Dogs run along the creek bed with the speed
of lightning chasing rabbits and squirrels.
This trail leads through a forest of pine,
fir, cedar and madrone; madrone who reaches
out her glorious arms as we pass.

This trail climbs the hill, three miles
above and down again.. A pair of hawks
circle overhead. The dogs bark and jump
after their imaginations. What could be
better than winter when the water is high?
What could be more fun?

Message in a Bottle

You don't know me
and I don't know you
but we are both living
on this great round ball
called Earth.

The year is 2020, the year
of fear. We all wear
masks over our faces
to protect ourselves
and those near us.

The masks hide our smiles.
As you read this, if
we were sitting together
on the sand,
we wouldn't be able

to recognize each other
in case we met
again someday. This
is not our only fear.
We have seen fires,

like we have never known
ravage our small towns.
People have lost their homes
Communities destroyed.
The result of climate change.

The world is heating up faster
than we can adapt, much less
prevent. Oceans are rising
Glaciers are melting. I have hope
that by the time

you are reading this,
we will have reached
some kind of balance
on this planet,
Our government

will no longer be run
by a clown. Our masks
will be removed and we
will smile at each other
and maybe even hug.

This letter is for you
From Joan Peterson, Autumn 2020

To Winter

Autumn dies away in gold
The heat of summer finally dimmed
Here comes winter trimmed in frost
Fanning out the sweating limbs.

Every morning trimmed in white
Branches sparkle with crystal beads
A new world covered in liquid drops
Ponds replenished, streams renewed.

December lies around the corner
Holiday season lurks once more
The crazy gifting, unending decor
Making up for lockdown indoors.

Away with winter my heart cries out
Bring me back that summer heat
Just as the world begins to thaw
I remember the fires, the stifling smoke.

I turn again to winter's quiet
The softness snow can bring to night.
I count the ways I love the world
When all is well in winter's light.

Pandemic

People are wearing masks
As an attempt to prevent
New and dangerous viruses
Directed out into the air
Even with social distancing
Making it seem safe
In going about our business
Carrying on our isolated lives.

Koji

We leave the old year behind,
the fires, the virus, the many conflicts
in our world. I watch the moon slip
behind the mountain, the light
fades and new life begins.

He is 2 feet tall, 10 months old, learning
to walk, he stands on the rocking horse
rails and balances. Tries to throw over
his leg, falls back on his bottom and laughs.

He blows bubbles, barks at the dogs
squeals at the cat, crawls through three
rooms in a minute. I run through the house
arms outstretched, trying to capture
the sun.

He brings in the New Year with light.
I leave dark times behind me and reach
for the future with love.
He is my light in the world.

Learning to Dance

He reaches out his arms, he wants to dance
He takes my hand, we spin around the room,
He's only one year old and full of grace.

We try a waltz a two step, a new pace
Any song will fill our one desire;
He holds onto my arms, he wants to dance.

When music starts to play we take a chance
We even feel the rhythm in our feet.
He's only one year old and full of grace.

We try a little spin for an advance
Across the room and off we twirl.
He reaches out his arms, he loves to dance.

This brings back thoughts of early days
When boys were shy and girls afraid.
He's only one year old and full of grace.

In later years when time has raced ahead
What memories will he have
Of reaching out his arms when we would dance
When he was one year old and full of grace?

Dizain on Spring

Just when we thought spring was here for keeps
Back into winter we flew in a hurry
Clouds blew around us the second week
While flowers were blooming in all of their glory.

Our shovels and rakes were stashed in a flurry
Seeds to be planted thrown back in their cases
We couldn't imagine how crazy this race is
Sometimes in Oregon this yearly dilemma
Often in one or two other places
We are ready for spring and crash into drama.

Post Pandemic

My friend calls it "post damnpanic"
He sings, "Where Have All the Flowers Gone"
And we walk toward the future.

Picture how we were before COVID-19.
Walking close, shaking hands, hugging,
Showing our whole face in a crowd.

Over the year we got used to
Social distancing, avoiding eye contact
Turning down invitations from friends.

Now we must relearn our social graces
Standing in line for tickets
In order to see a movie.

We reacquaint ourselves with family
Who we haven't seen for a year
The new baby just born or grandmother
Living out her time.

Now we know the price we pay
For neglecting the warnings
Of health. Take care of your neighbor
Take care of yourself.

VII

Christin Lore Weber

Poet's Statement:

As I lived through the year of pandemic solitude, writing poetry with the Applegate Poets, I realized that many prompts called forth memories from my young adult years as a Catholic nun. Not surprisingly, the skills I needed to live through this present time had been imparted to me by the style of life and teachings of that ancient monastic way: silence, order, focus on the moment at hand, meditation, nature as a communication of divine life and light, prayer alternating with work, study, respect for and contemplation of whatever presents itself, gratitude for simple things, compassion for those who suffer. As I watched what seemed a world coming apart, I found the writing of poetry to be a participation with all those whose lives were devoted to putting that world back together in new and creative ways. Through poetry it was possible to see through the present disintegration, gather the fragments, and reformulate them. I felt grateful for every poem, for each poet, and for the work that brought us through.

Silence at Slea Head

Clouds on this day between the times
Float above the Applegate
Soft closing over us like sleep,
While winds of yesterday speak low
Through backyard chimes,
Less sound than a deeper
Stillness

From a great long time ago,
The day as grey as sea foam
Swirling on the rocks at Slea Head
Where ghosts still pray,
As mystic silence swept all thought
Away.

While I sat quiet there
Upon a rock where purple heather bloomed,
Ocean winds lifted from a distant past
The God-crazed hermits' sinuous theophany of song.
I heard it echo off the stone
Of their now empty beehive huts
On the Skellig Islands, there to lose themselves,
To pray.

O, it wraps me still
In silence silver-grey
A flow that follows words
And frees the human soul
To be attuned for an awareness far more whole
Than any sound on earth
Could possibly
Convey.

Woman to Woman

Flesh is not bronze nor is strength made of stone,
One woman wrote her friend a thousand years ago
When springtime came with rain and illness in the home,
Food being scarce and herbs for healing low.

One woman wrote her friend a thousand years ago
As women will, in secret and by candlelight
Food being scarce and herbs for healing low,
Nurture stillness as they wait

As women will, in secret and by candlelight
Hold back from rage at seeds that failed to grow,
Nurture stillness as they wait
Beyond faith, hope and love for what they do not know.

Hold back from rage at seeds that failed to grow,
When springtime comes with rain and illness in the home,
Beyond faith, hope and love for what we do not know,
For flesh is not bronze nor is strength made of stone.

-with thanks to Clare of Assisi for the first and last lines.

Lace Makers

"Our lives should simply be an act of love."
—MAXIMS of the Sisters of St. Joseph.

They made lace;
Six widows from the sheer
Treacherous mountains of Le Puy
In south-central France,
Who in circa 1650 of the Lord
Made a vow to God.

With thread of finespun wool
And shuttle for the turning and the knotting it,
The widowed sisters plied their art,
A form of grace that they would give away,
Or sell for bread to feed the poor.
Illiterate but one, they worked the threads
Of their own ragged lives into patterns beautiful,
The humility of simple love and care.

Now that I am old maybe I see
The meaning that escaped me
More than sixty years ago
When I first cast my lot
With the daughters of those widows of Le Puy.
I am an intricacy in their design,
I am a fragment of their lace,

Whom on an August day
They gave away.

Home

Six degrees from home she wandered,
At least that, not counting dreams, in her search
For the very thing she wandered from, where she might fit
Each floor plan, making proper use of every room.
In dreams the dwelling places multiplied, surprising her
With spaces she discovered on the other side
Of tunnels made of stone that opened out
Into a great hotel, a boarding house, a place to stay a while,
But not a home.

As years, cities, countryside, and the eyes
Of strangers and of friends opened to receive
Her and whatever she could bring,
And as her heart also opened wider
To her wondering, to her deepening,
To her yearning for essential paradox
In the vision she contained,
Each further step required her to drop
Some perfect memory of all she sought,
An image she'd been treasuring.

How then would she know it
When she finally arrived? What if she'd let go
That unique, that necessary bit of its identity
The space in which she fit?
She could no longer calculate the distance she had come,
The loves holding, lifting, changing her,
Those she had lost. At evening she rested on a
        great dark stone
Beside the road. She put down everything.

Alone and filled with endless space,
The name of which she could not place although she knew
The feel of it, the sense, almost the voice
Of something now so near that distance was erased.
There could be no other place
Than in herself to find that home, that grace
To be, to live, to roam.

Dance

Tall, elegant and old
You reached out your slender hand to choose
Me. Did I know you? A trace of others
Over lifetimes flashed across your face,
In the angles of your stance,
Just so. How could I not know?
You seemed to fold
Your body with familiar grace
Like my mother's mother
When she turned in sunlight
From her gardening to place her hand
Upon my arm, as you did
In that empty space
That trance, a dream
Of music
Not yet
Played.

We prayed that dance,
Your old feet and mine
Together, in and out, like breath,
The folding of the universe
Upon itself
Like love,
And death.

Father Mother God

A variation on the form "Acrostic/Golden Shovel." Each line starts with the first letter of each word of the "Our Father" prayer and ends with consecutive words from the beginning stanza of "The Wreck of the Deutschland," by Gerard Manley Hopkins.

O Wisdom, dance of universal being, **Thou**
Flight of wings, infinite imagining, **mastering**
Within your sacred womb the form even of **me**,
Aloud I cry into the heart of all things—**God**!

Infinite beauty, source of truth, **giver**,
Heart of compassionate love, without which is
    no meaning **of**
Heaven that travels on our every **breath**.
Be with us Mother of all goodness, **and**
Throw your dough upon the board, knead
    your sacred **bread**,
Nourish the hungry bodies, minds and souls of our **world's**
Troubled peoples lost upon the **strand**,
Keening in the wild **sway**.
Cleanse us, Mother spirit **of**
The river stone, the rain, **the**
Whirlpools of your raging **sea**.
Be more to us than simply **Lord**;
Dive into the marrow **of**
Our bones; be one with us; our every moment's **living**
Energy, our flow of blood, our song, our birthing, **and**
All mystery gathered in the moment we are **dead**.

I stand before you, Mother Wisdom, O **Thou**
In wind, water, earth and air, Thou **hast**
Incarnated me. By you I am in body **bound**.
High lift me 'til the moon lights up my **bones**.
Gather each fragment of my earthly life, **and**
Undo tangles in my labyrinth of **veins**
To let me flow. Open my heart to let life **in**.

Deliver **me**,
O Splendor of Eternal Light that **fashioned**
Day, color, and the eyes of **me**.
Be praised in all **flesh**
Alive as hope in all we hold **and**
Feel in heartbeats, even touch with healing **after**
Understanding our fragility has failed. Renew **it**,
O Tender Infinite hidden in the spaces, **almost**
Trembling with power to bring forth the yet **unmade**
All. Lady Wisdom present in our depths, **what**
Wonders you have worked in us. **With**
Faith do we reach out beyond the **dread**
That haunts our dark, **Thy**
Womanly divinity, a velvet womb enclosing us, **doing**
The mathematics that divides the cells, **and**
Adds jewels of spirit and soul to our humanity, **Dost**
Unveiling of thy mystery discover you? **Thou**
Art the secret in the Source of Being, the **touch**
Lingering when we wake. Thou hast made a dream of **me**.

Untie, O Inanna, our ancient bonds so we can live **afresh**.
Night, O Layla, is your element once our dusk is **over**.
Infinity, Sophia, the spiral for your dance **again**.
Tree of Life, Eva, seeding each new **I**.
Blessing, Gaia, earth teaching hearts to **feel**.
Devotion, Demeter, to the eternal return of "**Thy**."
Unknowing, Erishkegal, the undoing in your **finger**.
Forgiveness, Isis, bringing back to life, **and**
Eternity, El. Grant us to **find**
Amen. May we inhabit **Thee**.

Beyond the Veil

The young nun's hair, before the sisters veiled it
in black wool,
Shone like a winter moon, and shimmered
Reminiscent of Isolde going forth, most beloved
Of us all, to meet the promised, the desired one.
We imagined that she walked among the berries
Red just beneath the snow, and her feet bare
But, by the miracle enclosing her, kept warm.
We imagined her reaching out her arms,
Light surrounding her, a Lover.

What harm could come to her, the chosen one?
But we were young. We took it as a mark of beauty
When her cheeks flushed and her eyes lowered;
When her fingers slipped to discord on the organ keys
We thought it pure humility. When she fled from us
To hide behind angelic pillars in the holy places
And cried out when she was found, we let her be,
Thinking her a visionary, one who could see
Wonders far beyond the souls of you or me.

We did not know the sign of illness that approaches
Under winter sky, silently, by stealth, by poison in
the air between
Our breath, our words, the movement of a hand, sly, a kiss.
Warnings began slowly to intensify. First, we were dry
Leaves that she would crush beneath her shoe,
Then she drew a serpent coiled round us as we huddled,
Aware suddenly the snake would strike. At last she
made it clear;
"You are right to fear. I'll gouge out each eye.
I'll kill you, dear."

The treatment meant to heal took most of her away.
How could she stay with us? Mind muddled, memory erased
In the shocking sway of electrodes to the brain. Why must
even goodness
Be susceptible to pain? Does something hunger to consume
Every part of us, matter and the mind; realms of soul;
Even the antechambers of the One Divine.

"There are other ways to serve beyond the veil,"
the abbess said.
"It is time to take that curve in the promises you made,
And flee round toward a kinder world where you can more
fully be."
Our young sister stood and reached for the long pin that
held the veil.
It slipped smoothly from the finely woven wool.
Light from the window shimmered through the weave.
The veil seemed not so heavy after all. Released,
The sunlit strands of her own natural hair streamed free.

Fissure

I inhabit spaces no one else has shared.
Since earliest moments I have entered there;
The fissure in the rock beside the river wide,
The stone cottage clinging to an edge of land
Whereon the lighthouse stood.
It's your imagination, Mama said,
Whenever fissures led me deep into a wood
Of tangled paths and caves of screams.

What is it holds me in its teeth?
The seduction of a world unseen,
The pull of a reality unknown, never-named,
The summons in the night by horror or by dream.

Once long ago I vowed the paradoxes of antiquity
Connecting me to laws that can organize a fissured world
Pillars that support this further realm
Where poverty yields substance,
Purity sustains,
And obedience unleashes an awakened will
To transform an unjust age
With the courage of a focused, self-transforming love.

Shall I remove my spirit from this fissured rock?
Shall I not follow its line of demarcation down
Past sensation into the imaginal,
The merging place where this is that,
Where blindness yields itself to sight
And the stone cottage on the fissure's edge
Is the house of light?

Convent Road

I walked with you
Between the field of wheat
And the apple orchard
To the sheepfold gate.
We opened it,
The latch a leather belt
Slipped across a pole.
Nature provided fencing;
River to the south, curving
Round to the backwash on the north.
A small flock cuddled in between.

I walked with you where wild asparagus grew
Among Jack in the Pulpit in the wetland
Down from the roadbed, and a red leaf
From the autumn past had been preserved
At the bottom of a lake in miniature,
Caught momentarily within a shaft of light.

We angled right
Into the trees.

You pointed out a thornbush
Growing low along the road,
Tiny cross-shaped thorns
Among red berries on the branch
Slender as a reed. It is the paradox,
You said.

Beyond the field of sugar beets
Close to the river
Where gooseberries grew,
And snails slimed their ambling way,

Stinging nettles canopied the path,
The beauty of their large leaves
Beckoning.

The narrow road you walked ahead of me
Ran along the river on a ledge
Twenty feet above the current's swirls,
And roots of ancient trees tangled, some torn
On the surface of the ground.
Trunks of maple and of elm leaned
Over the Red River of the North
With only those roots to hold their weight.
"I see Christ crucified
On this tree," you frightened me
As you leaned against the wood
Bent downward over the river-current's swirl,
Daring.

The path then led through old growth woods
Where we swung on vines that hung from trees
So large and full they turned the sunlight green.
We laughed like children
And I loved you.
Loved you.

One late afternoon you took all twenty-two of us
To a clearing on the road
Where the path ended in a grassy field;
We gathered fallen branches,
Stacked them in the center for a fire where we roasted corn.
We ate a simple supper,
And sat circled while you read to us
A mystic story of young women
In a land between the earth and sky.
The twenty-two of us lay down,
Our black veils spread like wings upon the grass.

Darkness fell. We sang every song we knew
As the stars appeared and sparks from the bonfire
Ascended upwards towards the Milky Way
To meet them.

Where might it end, this road?
I still feel torn roots beneath my feet,
Vines held in my hands, and from the pages of my Bible
I still lift a small red leaf, and gaze
Upon a tiny cross-shaped thorn.

Meditation

Leaves fall on the lake
Fragile boats floating towards shore
Dragonfly asleep

The green ferns uncurl
Galaxies of dewy stars
Morning symphony

On my lettuce leaf
Snail carries her spiral house
Watch out! Don't eat her.

Fawn grazes on dry grass
Mother of the whole herd
Walks away. Enough!

Midnight clear as noon
Goddess beams now fill my room
Aquarian full moon

Now I lay me down
In the living gold of Fall
Birch trees' yellow leaves.

Acknowledgements

The poets give grateful acknowledgment to the editors of the publications where a few of the poems in *Penned Up* first appeared.

Lisa E Baldwin

from The Historical Record
(First published in */pãn| dé| mïk/ 2020,* Oregon Poetry Association, 2021.)

Carpe Diem: Friday, November 13
(First published in *Truths and Consequences,* by Lisa E Baldwin. N8tive Run Press, 2021.)

Diana Coogle

To T. S. Eliot on the First Day of April, 2020
(First published in */pãn| dé| mïk/ 2020,* Oregon Poetry Association, 2021.)

To My Husband as He Lies Dying
(First published in *From Friend to Wife to Widow: Six Brief Years,* by Diana Coogle. Laughing Dog Press, 2020.)

H. Ní Aódagaín

This is a Time of Sorrow
(First published *in /pãn| dé| mïk/ 2020,* Oregon Poetry Association, 2021.)

Walking the Talk
(first published in *Applegater Community Newsmagazine,* Winter 2020.)

About the Poets

Lisa E Baldwin, a fifth-generation native Oregonian, works as a poet and freelance writer, an editor and publisher, a teacher, literary consultant, and poetry evangelist. Her poetry has been published in the *Jefferson Journal, Crosswinds Poetry Journal, The Applegater, Grants Pass Daily Courier,* several issues of *Verseweavers*, the *Encore Prize Poems 2020* and *2018*, and several regional anthologies. In April 2021, Baldwin launched N8tive Run Press and published her first book of poetry, *Truths and Consequences*.

Originally from Georgia, **Diana Coogle** has lived on the same mountainside in the Applegate since 1974. She was a Marshall Scholar at Cambridge University, earned a Ph. D. at age 68, and taught at Rogue Community College, University of Oregon, and Gothenburg University, Sweden. Her first compilation of public radio commentaries, *Fire from the Dragon's Tongue*, was an Oregon Book Award finalist. She published a book of poems, *From Friend to Wife to Widow: Six Brief Years*, in 2020

Beate Foit, originally from Germany, moved to the Applegate 17 years ago. She has been writing for over 30 years, primarily for her own enjoyment. A professional translator since 1984, she enjoys language in all its forms as books, plays, and songs. Some poems appeared online and in published anthologies. She joined the Applegate Poets in 2015 and has been reading selected poems and prose at Southern Oregon locations. Aside from writing poetry, Beate is writing stories about her life.

Seth Kaplan is a poet, community builder, and resident of the Applegate Valley. His heart is taking the shape of the place he lives, and he is blessed to share the experience with Lily, Shayna, Sweet Pea, and an unfolding community. His poems have appeared in *From the Heart of the Applegate, Oakland Renaissance, Peralta Art & Literary Journal, Good News, Peralta Press, Sonoma Mandala, Open Hand,* and other publications lost to time.

H. Ní Aódagaín is a writer of fiction, poetry and essay. Her work explores the power of women, the challenge of living consciously on this beautiful and beleaguered planet we call home, and the role of the individual to make change for the better of all. Her writings have appeared in *Autostraddle, Eureka Literary Magazine, Leaping Clear, Oregon Quarterly, Sinister Wisdom,* and most recently, in */pãn/dé/mïk/ 2020*. Please visit her website at hnauthor.com or email hnauthor@gmail.com.

Joan Peterson retired from teaching writing classes at Rogue Community College several years ago. She lives on a farm in Applegate, Oregon where she finds time to walk, garden, sing and write. She has published her work in *Intricate Homeland (2000), West Wind Review, Rogues' Gallery, Oregon English Journal, Fireweed,* and other literary magazines. She has one chapbook of poems, *Brilliant By the Door(1999),* and a published book of poems, *Looking for a Place to Write (2014).*

A multi-genre author, **Christin Lore Weber** has been published by traditional presses large and small. Scribner's, Simon&Schuster, HarperCollins, Loyola University Press, Yes, International Publications, Innisfree Press and others. She and her husband John R. Sack now publish under their own imprint, CyberScribe Publications. The interrelationship of human with divine has been her enduring theme in all genres, the power of story her fascination, and paradox in existence her signature pattern both in writing and living.

Appendix A:
A SELECTION OF PROMPTS

Most of the poems in this volume were written in response to the 100+ prompts shared within our group during the pandemic lockdown. The prompts listed here are those that sparked at least two poems selected for inclusion in *Penned Up*.

April 1, 2020 Write a welcome letter to April, the "cruellest month" according to T.S. Eliot.
Pages 24, 68,

April 14, 2020 Write a Pantoum.
Pages 38, 101

April 22, 2020 Today is the 50th Earth Day celebration. Write a prayer, a gratitude, or perhaps a love poem for our home planet.
Pages 39, 72

August 23, 2020 *To Look at Anything* by John Moffitt offers us a theme: That which is unseen.
Pages 28, 41

September 18, 2020 Write about the sorrow we are currently all feeling, and address all the loss, real and potential.
Pages 43, 75, 86

October 23, 2020 Write a poem that would be a message in a bottle: your last will and testament, a note to an unrequited lover, or a secret that you have kept for many years.
Pages 32, 89

November 14, 2020 Write a golden shovel poem and, if you can, make it an acrostic poem as well.
Pages 18, 27, 104

November 27, 2020 Can we find the beauty in winter, a season some find hard to live through? Write an ode to winter.
Pages 33, 91

December 4, 2020 Create a poem based on a recipe… but not necessarily for food.
Pages 16, 46

January 16, 2021 Write a Korean Sijo poem which follows a structure similar to Japanese Haiku and Tanka.
Pages 47, 84

January 30, 2021 Write about walking on a familiar trail in nature.
Pages 34, 88, 109

February 20, 2021 Listen to a piece of music that you love. Let the music inspire the poem.
Pages 36, 96

February 27, 2021 Write a poem based on this timely little quote from Margaret Atwood: *"In the Spring, at the end of the day, you should smell like dirt."*
Pages 48, 95

April 11, 2021 Consider Space, our moon, Mars, stars, The Milky Way, uncountable galaxies, black holes, worm holes, light years…
Pages 49, 56

April 15, 2021 Is today the Ides of April? Is there such a thing? I think it is so. Make a poem prompted by ideas about magic and witches and wizards and spells and charms and hocus-pocus of all sorts. And since it is April, throw in some windy, stormy weather.

Pages 20, 59

April 17, 2021 Two quotes to consider, and then let them take you where they will:
"All happy families resemble one another; each unhappy family is unhappy in its own way." —Leo Tolstoy in *Anna Karenina* and "Home is the place where, / when you have to go there, / they have to take you in." — Robert Frost in *The Death of the Hired Man*

Pages 54, 101

April 20, 2021 Write a "working class" poem. Maybe it says something about the Labor Movement, or economic justice, or maybe it is a character poem about someone you know/ knew.

Pages 29, 62

April 24, 2021 Write a spring garden poem, one that carries ideas of renewal and rebirth.

Pages 13, 60

Appendix B:
POETIC FORMS, STYLES, AND DEVICES

As we Applegate Poets are students of poetry as well as practitioners of the craft, we often experiment with various aspects of poetics. Listed here are the definitions and explanations of some forms, styles, and devices we played with during the pandemic.

Acrostic The first letter of each line, read down, spells a name or other word.
Pages 18, 92

Allusion as basis Basing one poem on extended references to another
Pages 15, 24, 33, 104

Blank verse Unrhymed stanzas in iambic pentameter (10 syllables per line, usually iambic, i.e., one unstressed syllable followed by one stressed syllable)
Page 36

Catalogue A list poem, often using anaphora (repeated word at the beginning of a line)
Pages 29, 75

Corona (or crown) Haiku A new poetic form, developed by Lisa Baldwin as a prompt for August 8, 2020, which she defines as "a sequence of five stanzas in haiku form plus an ending couplet, totaling seventeen lines overall (to echo the 17 syllables in a haiku). A recurring image links the sections of the poem, a nod to the origins of haiku in the *renga*, another Japanese form. The two lines in the couplet must rhyme and must be seven syllables each in length to create coherence with the haiku's middle line. The 14-syllable count in the couplet echoes the 14-line structure of sonnets."
Pages 17, 40

Dizain A 10-line poem, with 10 (sometimes 8) syllables in each line and a rhyme scheme of a-b-a-b-b-c-c-d-c-d. The rhyme scheme sometimes varies.

Pages 48,95

Elegy A poem exploring loss and consolation

Pages 52, 98

Epistolary A poem written in the form of a letter to someone

Page 24

Erasure poem A type of found poem created by erasing words in another text, leaving a poem entirely different from the original text

Page 87

Free verse A Poem that does not have a patterned rhyme scheme nor a regular meter

Pages 14, 21, 78 + (Many poems in this collection are written in free verse.)

Golden Shovel Each line ends with a word from another poem or song lyric or even a short prose excerpt, which, read down, reveals a complete line from that other work.

Pages 18, 27, 104

Haiku A Japanese poetic form consisting of three lines: the first of five syllables, the second of seven syllables, and the third of five syllables. A traditional haiku uses a seasonal reference and a *kireji*, or "cutting word," a sharp turn or surprise, usually in the last line of the poem

Page112

Internal rhyme Rhymed words within lines rather than at the ends

Page 34

Lyric A short poem, often with songlike qualities, that expresses the speaker's personal emotions and feelings
Pages 12, 88, 108

Narrative style A poem that tells a story
Pages 76, 100, 106, 109

Nonet A nine-line poem with descending number of syllables in each line, beginning with nine syllables in the first line, eight in the second, and so on to the last one-syllable line
Page 45

Ode A poem in praise of a person or object or place
Pages 33, 56, 74, 91

Poem for two voices A poem written as a dialogue between two entities—people, places, things, or ideas—that presents two different points of view. The two speakers are often presented on either side of the page.
Page 82

Quatrain A four-line poem or stanza, often using alternating rhyme: abab, cdcd, etc.
Page 31

Pantoum A sixteen-line poem of four unrhymed quatrains with repeated lines in a set format:
Stanza one: lines 1, 2, 3, 4
Stanza two: lines 2, 5, 4, 6
Stanza three: lines 5, 7, 6, 8
Stanza four: lines 7,3,8,1
The pantoum is a Malay poetic form, used in French and English.
Pages 38, 99

Sijo A Korean poetic form using three lines of between 14 and 16 syllables each, for a total syllable count of 44–46 syllables. The rhythm and lilt of each line is determined by whatever grouping pattern the poet decides to use, only keeping the total syllable count for the line the same. Typically, each line will also use a caesura, a break or a pause in the middle of the thought. The word sijo means "the melody of the times."

Pages 47, 84

Sonnet A 14-line poem in rhymed iambic pentameter (10 syllables per line, usually iambic, i.e., one short [unstressed] syllable followed by one long [stressed] syllable) in either of two forms:

Shakespearean:

three quatrains (four-line stanzas)
and a closing couplet
rhyme scheme of abab, cdcd, efef, gg

Petrarchan

one octave (eight-line stanza)
with rhyme scheme abbaabba
and one sestet (six-line stanza)
with variations of the cde rhyming lines

Pages 19, 26

Villanelle A highly structured poem, originally French, made of five tercets (three-line stanzas), followed by a quatrain (four-line stanza), and using only two rhymes, repeated in a given pattern. The first and third lines of the first stanza repeat alternately as refrain lines in the following stanzas' third lines and the last two lines of the closing quatrain.

Page 94

www.ingramcontent.com/pod-product-compliance
Ingram Content Group UK Ltd.
Pitfield, Milton Keynes, MK11 3LW, UK
UKHW041640190726
13854UKWH00006B/2608